GRATITUDE RENEWED

A Journey Journal

De Miller and Mark Miller

MillerWords
PO Box 1622
Mount Dora, FL 32756

This book is a work of fiction. The names, characters,
places, and incidents are products of the writer's
imagination or have been used fictitiously and are not to be
construed as real. Any reference to historical events, real
people or real places are used fictitiously. Any resemblance
to persons, living or dead, actual events, locales or
organizations is purely coincidental.

Copyright © 2015 by De Miller, Mark Miller

Edited by Susan O'Gara

First Edition

For discounts on bulk purchases, please contact MillerWords Educational
Sales at **Sales@MillerWords.com**

Printed in the United States of America

2 4 6 8 10 9 7 5 3 1

Library of Congress Control Number: 2015904652

ISBN: 978-0692412374

INTRODUCTION

I have known De Miller for about seven years. I know him to be a man of very strong faith. When he talks about his movies, he gets very emotional. I believe this is because he feels God's presence and knows God is really moving his fingers on the keys. Otherwise, I cannot explain how he writes them so fast.

Over the years, I have learned about De's life. He worked as an investigative reporter for some time and met Sue in the early eighties. After they were united in marriage, De began to explore other creative jobs. There have been many ups and downs in the last thirty years, but they have pulled through. It was not until De gave his life to the Lord, about nine years ago, that he said he felt real peace and found a calling with his movie ministry.

I met Mark Miller, De's Son, about two years ago. Mark produces an author event called "Authors in the Park", which is really a showcase for local authors. De and Mark were sharing a table, with their books on display. I could see immediately that they had a real bond and respect for each other.

Since those days, De is now facing a major health issue. Though serious, I have never seen De's faith waver. He is strong in the Lord and continues to live with his spirits high.

For me to discuss this book, I would like to first talk about De's movie ministry, and in particular, the movie that inspired the book you are holding.

We never start a day of production without starting with prayer. "God, Where Are You?" was no exception.

I did not go to all of the shoots because I housed four of the crew. I tried to plan meals for them - it was not easy, due to their schedules. Sometimes, we ate between 5-6 p.m. so they could get to the shoot by 7:30p.m. They would not get home until early morning. They would eat breakfast and then sleep for a few hours.

We were shooting the movie during cold weather, mostly in February. Most shoots were done at night and some lasted until four in the morning. We had to shoot when the diner was closed. Of course, there were always retakes!! Some shots had to be outdoors, so we always had hot coffee and cocoa ready to keep us warm. The man who owned the diner left fritters for our snacks. Of course, De always had his "Moon Pies"!

At the diner, the traffic noise made it hard to get the sound correct. So we would try as much as possible to wait for a few trucks to go by and start filming. It didn't always work. The same thing happened when we were filming outside the Methodist church in Mt. Dora. That main street is busy, even late at night. We had one camera catty corner across the street and one in the front of the building we used. During the scenes where Sonny got into the preacher's ex-wife's car, we had both cameras on opposite corners. Later, we moved both over in front of the church annex building we were using as a temporary production office. The sound guys had their equipment in a little trailer around the corner of the building. We had cords strung all over.

This was the kind of creativity and determination that I came to expect from De. He would not let little, or even big, challenges stand in the way of the Message. I feel we were blessed, especially during this production.

One night, we had our usual two cameras rolling. During the set up for one of the scenes, De's wife Sue suddenly said, "Look at the wall!"

They looked at a normally blank yellow wall and there was an unmistakable image. It appeared to be a man with a beard wearing a long robe. Now, Christ did not have a beard that we know of, but that is a universal representation with which many are familiar. I wish I had been on set that night.

Not unlike the production, I see the story of "God, Where Are You?" as inspirational for all who feel they are down and out with no hope. Maybe they feel life has dealt them a blow and they never blame themselves. They look for someone else to blame and God is an easy target. To me, that means they do not truly believe anyway.

For those who believe in God, through the Lord Jesus Christ, we know there is a plan for our lives, even though we do not understand how God is going to use our misfortunes for His Glory. Psalms 32:7. Without spoiling the end of the movie, it shows us how unexpected God's plans can be. We may easily end up somewhere far from where we ever intended, but it may have always been His plan.

But for those who do not believe in God, or are mad at Him, they become depressed, angry and completely lost. This is the story of the main character Sonny. And this is where God comes in. He uses His believers (Angels) to reach out to those who need him most. Sonny meets Malachi who gives him a book called "Gratitude Renewed". Sonny has a seemingly simple task of writing in his journal. He soon finds that it is not so easy and it is this challenge that makes it all the more worthwhile.

As De is always thinking of new ways to spread God's word, it did not surprise me that he wanted to take the fictional book out of his movie and bring it into the real world. At first I thought it was supposed to be a book of devotionals, but, after reading it, I discovered it to be something more. Like Sonny does in the movie, this book can be used to keep track of true spiritual needs, instead of superficial, material wants. When a person allows God to forgive his transgressions and starts to see how God has, and will continue, to help him the more hope he has. Romans 5:1-5 NIV

Even if your life is "on track", this personal journal may give you some new perspectives. If you are facing troubles in your life, I think this book will be a helpful tool, but do not stop here.

In short, De Miller is a Christian man of strong faith. He wants to use the talents given to him by God to spread His message of salvation. His talent is in writing and making Christian films. I have been associated with De on his last five movies and find each one better than the previous.

I believe this book comes from their hearts and experiences. God is in charge!!

Phyllis Chapman
Executive Producer
Lazarus Filmworks

CHAPTER ONE

IT'S THE LITTLE THINGS…

Why does God let bad things happen to good people?

For that matter, why does God let bad things happen at all?

Unfortunately *this* is not *that* book. It is doubtful *that* book exists, because God simply does not answer *WHY?*

Of course, many times in life, it seems that we are overwhelmed with so-called *bad things.* God never promised, in His word, that we would have a trouble-free life here on earth.

A case could be made to show that we are the cause of all of our troubles here on earth, and that is not *we* specifically. That is *WE* collectively, as inhabitants of this earth.

In the beginning, God intended for us humans to have no troubles. Our ancestors,

Adam and Eve had only to obey God's one directive. Had they done that, we would be living in paradise still. But, you no doubt know how that concluded. Because of Adam and Eve's disobedient acts, sin was brought into this world and it's been an ongoing battle ever since.

So, is there an answer to the *why* question? No, there is no answer. That's not very satisfying is it?

But, if you will follow the suggestions found in the pages of this book and fill it up with your own personal story, you should have a better understanding of the *why* and a deeper understanding of your own faith.

The first step on this journey, and a continuing assignment throughout this book, is to be grateful for what you do have. By doing this one simple thing, you will soon see that you do, indeed, have way more for which to be grateful. Soon, your gratitude will outweigh your questions.

Throughout this book, we will examine some personal testimonies of actual people. We will, however, change the names so that we can get closer to the *why* and not be distracted with the *who*.

First, we will look at David.

David was a young man working at a very nice job in the career field for which he had trained. He had a very happy life. He was married to his high school sweetheart and they had two young children. They lived in a nice neighborhood, drove nice cars and had nice friends. Everything was nice.

Then, it became not so nice. It was downright B-A-D. David's wife acted out an all-too-familiar scene when she ran away with David's best friend. The sun, in David's world at least, stopped shining. Everything fell apart.

David searched for answers. He did nothing wrong; yet, this *bad* thing happened to HIM! Why? He asked everyone. Why was his life in shambles? Why was everything gone? Why did he have nothing left?

In a later chapter we will look at a piece of advice that helped David get back on track. But for now, we're going to look at *the little things.*

Finally, one day, David started to realize that the *why* really did not matter. He saw that even if he got that question answered, his life would be exactly the same. Nothing would change. So he started looking around for things to do, at least to keep his mind busy.

One of the things he did, after coming home from work each day, was to run around the track at the local junior high school. Imagine, if you will, the world without an iPod. David had no iPod to listen to tunes as he ran and walked around the quarter mile track. One day, after a particularly good day at his job, as he was walking around the track he said, out loud to himself, "At least I still have my job. I love my job. At least that wasn't taken away from me."

As he continued around the track he started to realize that, because he replaced only one of the negative thoughts he had been thinking about his life with the positive thought about his job, he felt better. It was a strange feeling that he had not felt in a long while. He actually felt better because he was grateful he still had the job that he loved.

The next day, during his run, he thought about his job again, simply because it made him feel a little bit better. But the second day, he also thought about his children and how wonderful it was that he still had his children.

As the days passed, he continued to add things to his list. Things that he was grateful he still had. Things that he had all along. Things that he had *not* lost.

As his continued his daily regime around the track, he so looked forward to the time that he challenged himself to add more and more to his list. Some of the other people who were also using the track gave him sideways glances as he walked and ran and talked to himself.

"I am grateful for my job. I am grateful for my children. I am grateful for my home. I am grateful for my car. I am grateful for...," he continued. As his workouts got longer, his list got longer, until he was talking about things like the 27 inch television in his bedroom and the collection of Beatles' albums he had.

Then, one miraculous day, the sun came up in David's world. And what put it there? Being grateful for *the little things*.

We all have them. It might be hard to make a list now, but concentrate. Think. Remember. Try it now. And keep it up.

Assignment Number 1

Fill these next few pages with every one of the things you do have. Things you are grateful you still have in your life. We'll start you with a freebie.

I am grateful for being alive.

I am grateful for...

Journal

Journal

Journal

Journal

CHAPTER TWO

FORGIVE OTHERS

Luke said it best – "...I say to you who hear, love your enemies, do good to those who hate you..." (Luke 6:27)

Those are simple words. The meaning is clear and direct. You have started your journey and now you have a direction to take. For most, this will be the easiest chapter and that makes for a great first step.

In that quote, Luke is talking about love. Forgiveness is one way to show that love.

Giving forgiveness is something that can be private or public. It is something you do in mind, heart and action. You can even send it in an email (but that's kind of like cheating).

The best way to forgive someone is by saying the words. There are people in your life that you feel have wronged you in some way. Many times, these are painful or embarrassing situations. Sometimes, it turns out that you held it in your heart, while the other person had no clue how it affected you. It may take some courage to speak to the person.

When you look into someone's eyes and say, "I forgive you," you will see what it means to them. Pain and ill will can lift instantly, but not always. In some cases, it will take time for the other person to process and accept your forgiveness.

It is a two-way street. In almost every situation, the people who wronged you likely feel that you have done the same to them. (More about that in Chapter Four). If you walk up to someone and randomly forgive them without any explanation or context, you might be greeted with a blank stare – or worse.

What happens if the person has no idea to what you are referring? What if your sudden, unannounced proclamation makes the situation worse? What if the person has already left this world?

Those are important questions. Let's look at each one.

The clueless person does not know they wronged you. Yet, for years, you have held a grudge and avoid them at the office, or on the street. Whatever caused the situation, it is only known to you, in your mind and heart. A person, who does not know his or her misdeed, is not likely to accept your forgiveness.

The grudge holder is even more challenging. If you offer your forgiveness to someone who is not ready to accept it – or give you their own forgiveness – then your words are only going to make things worse. You have now stirred up old feelings, resentment, maybe even hatred. This is like pulling the scab off a scraped knee before the cut is fully healed. You are back to the beginning when you were only trying to resolve it.

Lastly, how do you forgive someone who has passed away? This answer actually applies to the first two groups as well. True forgiveness is given in your heart. You cannot speak to the dead with your mouth. However, God knows your heart. He knows your thoughts and feelings. Even when it is difficult, or impossible, to say the words out loud, you have to honestly hold the forgiveness in your heart.

The seed of forgiveness comes from within you. Words are easy. Truth is difficult. Not everyone can readily say what they think or feel. The next chapter discusses this more.

Let forgiveness begin with you. Each of us has our own journey and when your "offender" is ready, their acceptance and forgiveness will come back to you.

Assignment Number 2

This will be an honest, and long, list. Write down names of people that you believe have done you wrong. Include those who have passed away. This list will include physical wrongs (if you were the victim of a crime) and emotional wrongs (the kid that made fun of your braces in middle school).

Journal

Journal

Journal

Journal

Journal

CHAPTER THREE

SELF-FORGIVENESS

The self – our own best friend and our own worst enemy.

No one on this material earth knows what we hold in our hearts and minds. There is One who does and ultimately, that is all that matters.

This is where we come back to our friend David. You will see in a later chapter how he came to this point. It is a journey, not a magic pill. There are steps to take. However, we will discuss self-forgiveness here between giving forgiveness and asking forgiveness.

Everything starts with the self. That is how we define our world. I, I, I...me, me, me...

I believe, I think, I feel. That is who we are – our tastes, our physical traits, our likes and dislikes. That is where forgiveness starts. Before you can give forgiveness to others, you have to believe it and hold it in your heart. If you are guilty of something or believe you have done something wrong, how can you move past it without forgiving yourself?

David came to a point in his journey where he needed to realize that. Since the day his wife left him, he asked himself, "What did I do wrong? Why is this happening to me?"

In this case, did David do something wrong? Did he deserve to lose his perfect life? No, he was not the unfaithful one. Maybe some of his actions led to a weakened marriage, but ultimately the blame in this situation did not fall on him. Still, David felt like he had sinned in some way.

Before David could experience gratitude renewed, he had a major hurdle to overcome. He had to forgive himself. Like the song from the popular animated movie, he had to "let it go".

1 John 1:9 says, "If we confess our sins, He is faithful and just to forgive us our sins

and to cleanse us from all unrighteousness."

Did David visit a confessional and say his Hail Mary's? Even if he did, it would have no meaning until he opened his heart to God. It is what is inside of us that needs to be forgiven. We have to forgive ourselves for God to forgive us. Matthew 6: 14-15 does say that if we forgive others, then we are forgiven. So this may seem to contradict that. However, are we not all part of this world? It is reasonable to think that as we forgive our fellow man, we must include ourselves in that. As long as we hold on to greed, covetousness or anger, we will not be free to continue our journey.

Let it go.

We all sin. That is human nature. When we forgive ourselves, we are honestly asking God for forgiveness. It is a pact we make with Him. In order for all of the other parts of the plan to work, we have to start with a good, clean foundation. An open heart is that foundation. Forgiving others and forgiving ourselves gets things started. In the next chapter, you will see how asking for forgiveness goes beyond a silent prayer to God asking Him to wipe our slate clean.

Assignment Number 3

Be honest. Some day in the future you might want to share your journey with someone else (maybe even the new You). This list is about the pain you hold in your heart. Write about the things that make you feel guilty or angry. Write about your unresolved transgressions and things that are holding you back. No one said this would be easy.

Journal

Journal

Journal

Journal

CHAPTER FOUR

ASKING FORGIVENESS

For many, this may prove to be the most difficult chapter.

The reason being is that in order to ask forgiveness from others, you have to first admit you are wrong.

Whether accidentally or on purpose, in another's life or in your heart, you may have hurt someone. In order to fix this, you have to take the first step. This is an opportunity to take an inventory of your life. Maybe you have avoided someone because you wronged him or her in some simple way or you once had an unpleasant word. Maybe it was something minor, but maybe it was something major that ruined a relationship or changed your life.

The easy part is identifying these instances. Is there a person you don't answer when their number shows on your Caller ID? Is there someone you lied to? Or worse? These things can be real actions or thoughts and feelings.

Giving forgiveness can be personal and private. Asking forgiveness is something you are going to share with the world. At the very least, the person you are asking will have to know. Before you approach this person, you need to know why you are doing it.

Dealing with things that you left in the past may be difficult and even painful to revisit. Recall the circumstances and only move forward if you are truly repentant. You may not realize it, but you are carrying these things around like Ebenezer Scrooge's weights and chains.

The good news is that once you complete this chapter, you will start to feel those dragging chains fall away. You will be living a blame-free life. Forgive yourself, forgive others and then receive your own forgiveness. You will feel freer and you will feel lighter.

In a way, it is like a reset button. We all had "Do Overs" when we played kickball in grade school. Unfortunately, in adult life, we do not usually get a do over. This is as close as you can get. You cannot change the past, but you can be penitent for it. Then, when God looks into your heart, He sees your true self. The reason you feel lighter is because He is lifting you – bringing you closer to Him.

Remember David, from the first chapter?

David's oldest daughter, Sonya, never understood the circumstances of her parents' separation. She only saw things from David's point of view before he discovered the good left in his life. In a way, Sonya blamed her mother for changing their family. As Sonya entered her pre-teen years, she stopped accepting her mother's phone calls and would not even open her letters.

Sonya did not speak to her mother in over four years.

The great thing about gratitude renewed is that it is contagious. As David continued on his journey, it affected Sonya. At the age of sixteen, she realized something. Her best friend's mother passed away in a car accident. This made Sonya realize that, if she wanted, she could still pick up the phone and call her mother. She could ask for help or tell her she loved her. Sonya did that.

However, she did something even more mature for her age. When she reconnected with her mother, she started by asking forgiveness. She was the one that closed her mother out and she felt truly sorry for that.

When you start the list for this chapter, only write names and things for which you are truly sorry. If you are not ready to forgive yourself for something, then you are not ready to ask others to free you from it. Start with the little things. Start with people closest to you. Some people may not be ready to forgive you – that does not change what is in your heart. They have to adjust their own attitudes. Once you have freed yourself, others will see this and it will become easier for them to forgive you. As the little things drop away, the big things will start to break down on their own. Do not stop because someone does not instantly forgive you. They have to come to terms with it in their own way and everything moves on God's time.

Assignment Number 4

Here is a good place to start:

"I am sorry for..."

Journal

Journal

Journal

Journal

Journal

CHAPTER FIVE

GIVING

What does giving have to do with gratitude? Don't you usually show gratitude when you receive?

Have you ever heard the phrase *it is better to give than to receive*?

Giving has quite a lot to do with your own personal peace and satisfaction. What would a chapter about giving be without this verse:

"For God so loved the world, that he gave his only Son, that whoever believes in him should not perish but have eternal life." John 3:16

You have seen that sign at every major sporting event. John 3:16. What does it mean? It means that *it is better to give than receive.*

Really? No kidding?

Think about it. God loved the world (that includes us living in it) so much that he gave his ONLY Son. Is there anything for which you would sacrifice one of your children, or pets, or favorite book?

That is a lot of love. And what did God expect in return? Nothing. In fact, He gives even more. The deal is simple and beautiful. He gives His Beloved Son to be sacrificed, we believe and then He gives us eternal salvation.

So, start giving. Give your house to the homeless. Give your food to the hungry.

No, wait a minute. That is not what it means. If you can live a life without material possessions, then you are far better off than any advice this book can offer. Until we go on to claim our final reward, we all have to live in this world. 2 Corinthians 9:7 explains it better, "Each one must give as he has decided in his heart, not reluctantly or under compulsion, for God loves a cheerful giver."

Give what you can. Give your time and give your love. Share your knowledge and faith. Maybe you subconsciously realize that you have already been doing this –

forGIVE others, forGIVE yourself. As you progress along your journey, giving becomes automatic. The more gratitude you have, the more you will want to share it.

"The point is this: whoever sows sparingly will also reap sparingly, and whoever sows bountifully will also reap bountifully," 2 Corinthians 9:6.

Giving can be a very private thing. It should not ever be used to draw attention to yourself.

Hazel came from a wealthy family. In her later years her health and finances failed her. Every Sunday, she still made it to church and every Sunday, she gave her tithe. She thought about her four hundred dollar Social Security check. She calculated her electric bill and grocery budget. Then she put more than she could afford into her tithe without a word. All the while, she watched Mr. Jennings in the front pew. He usually made a show of kissing his envelope or clearing his throat as he dropped it in the collection basket.

When Hazel passed away from complications, including malnutrition, her pastor gave a eulogy that told how much she enjoyed watching the church basketball team. It gave her great pleasure and reminded her of her youth.

After her funeral, the collection plate seemed a little lighter. The sports program had to stop due to a lack of funds. Hazel's pastor discovered that her anonymous donation each week almost single-handedly supported the basketball team.

Can we all be Hazel? No. We do not always have money to give and it is not always about the money. This is not a free pass for getting out of the weekly tithe. For your church to continue its work, that tithe is important. However, even without that money, we can be *like* Hazel. We can give a little extra in other ways, whether it is attention, time or compassion.

Assignment Number 5

Here is a challenging list. What are things that you can give? Write down your talents and skills. Make a list of people that you can give something to. This list should NOT include any material donations – not money or possessions.

I am good at reading and writing – I can volunteer at my local library.

Journal

Journal

Journal

Journal

Journal

CHAPTER SIX

ACCEPTANCE

How many times have you heard the words, "Accept it"?

Maybe your mother said it to you when you were little? You wanted that cookie before dinner and she said no. You have to accept it. Maybe your boss said it to you when he called for mandatory overtime?

That's the way of the world. You have to accept it.

That's not exactly the point of this chapter. Acceptance has a broader meaning. It's about knowing yourself and being comfortable with the world as it is. It is also about realizing what you have, seeking what you need and casting away what is coveted.

It states in *John 6:37*, "All that the Father giveth me shall come to me; and him that cometh to me I will in no wise cast out." Think about that. It is not the cookie or the overtime. It is what God provided for you. It is right under your nose. It is the children you raise, the friends you keep and the food you eat. God gives us each what we can handle and no more. We are all worthy of His love and we start with that. Each thing in our life after that is ours, for better or worse.

Now it sounds like a marriage. In a way, it is. We are married to our life. For better or worse, for sickness and health. Good or bad, everything happens the way it is supposed to happen.

You ate one too many cookies and now you have diabetes. You refused to work the mandatory overtime and now you lost your job. You have to accept what is in your life.

That is not to say you should come to expect misery in everything. We all have our ups and downs. The acceptance part is how you deal with it – your attitude.

Richard is a retired soldier. He is also receiving disability payments because he has no legs. He lost them to a hidden explosive in a foreign country. In high school, Richard played soccer. He dreamed of playing in the World Cup. Losing a dream like that, in the way he did, would make someone bitter and resentful, right?

Not so for Richard. Almost from his first days of physical therapy, Richard accepted his situation. He knew he would never play soccer again, but he also knew his loss saved the lives of three other soldiers. Those soldiers were his friends and they still are today.

Think of the Serenity Prayer. There is a reason why it is the touchstone of so many groups, like Alcoholics Anonymous. The prayer calls for serenity, courage and wisdom. There is serenity in acceptance (more about that in chapter seven). So, we find peace in accepting what we cannot change, the things outside of us. Then we need courage to face what we can change. And last comes the wisdom to know the difference. The thing about being wise is that you do not have to accept everything. Don't forget, there is a difference between tolerance and acceptance.

You can improve your health and the safety of your neighborhood, but can you cure cancer? Under the right circumstances, maybe yes. However, generally, this is something we cannot change. Then how is it fair and why do we have to accept something like infant leukemia? Or what about a drunk driver that crashes into and kills a newlywed couple? Or worse?

The answer is simple, yet profound. There is sin in the world. From the first bite of the forbidden fruit, we are flawed. This does not have to be a sin you committed, but because sin is in the world, it affects us all.

We have to accept sin. We do not have to add to it. So, relax.

Realize that before you were conceived, God laid out His plan for you. Accept the good and bad in your life as part of God's greater plan. The ups and downs will happen when they are supposed to happen.

Now, it is your chance to make a list. Think about the things in your life that you cannot change. Don't make a "good" list and a "bad" list. Combine everything and maybe you will see how the peaks and valleys make for a beautiful landscape.

Assignment Number 6

Accept what is in your life. What do you have to accept physically, emotionally, mentally?

Journal

Journal

Journal

Journal

Journal

CHAPTER SEVEN

STAY CALM

You are getting things ready for a visitor. This is the last-minute panic clean of the house. Rush around, stuff things in drawers and closets.

Guess what? Your visitor has already seen your house the way you really keep it. Your visitor has always been there. Sometimes you ignore your visitor, which is not the sign of a good host at all.

Relax.

You know who the visitor is and you know that *He* is not worried about the cleanliness of your house. He does care about the cleanliness of your life. Forgiveness in all forms, giving and acceptance are the last-minute cleaning details while we get ready for the visitor that we forgot is already there.

Once you have made it this far in the book, serenity should already be part of your life. When those old debts are paid and you have accepted everything else, what you are left with is peace.

You are "too blessed to stress".

Psalm 37:7 says, "Be still before the Lord and wait patiently for Him."

Think about God's plan. It was written before the stars exploded across the sky, but contains the details of your life. Realize how special that makes you. Find peace in your salvation and know that the problems of this life are truly insignificant on a cosmic scale.

The point of this book is not the quick clean for a weekend visit. It is the deep cleaning of a lifetime commitment. There is more to it than a clean slate.

Being at peace yields its own rewards. It gives you clarity of vision.

You rush to get to work. You rush to get the kids to school. Rush, rush, rush. If you move as fast as a hummingbird, what are the chances of seeing one? When you are calm and still, you can watch that hummingbird dart about the way it was intended. Take time to look for the beauty in the world. It is everywhere, not only in nature. God put ideas into man's head and that beauty is seen in human design and performance. Beauty can be a uniquely designed building, a classical painting or even a juggling street performer.

That vision goes further. You will still face difficulties in your life. You already accept that. However, if you deal with them from a place of peace, they will not seem so insurmountable. If you sat in a small boat in the middle of the ocean, the only way to see the shore is on a flat, calm surface. A raging, wave-crested sea is no way to approach any problem. Or worse, you could suddenly be surrounded by unseen problems and head straight for the shallow rocks, smashing your boat to pieces.

Mattie wanted to grow a garden. She needed to save money on the grocery bill for her family and decided a garden would be the best way. She ran outside and tore up her back yard. She grabbed a few tools and seed packets from her local hardware store. She tore open each of the envelopes and jammed the seeds into the ground. Without checking the forecast each day, she flooded the garden with water. In a couple weeks, she had a few sprouts, but they were scattered and never produced anything.

Mattie could not understand why.

In her hurried, worried state, she made many mistakes.

It turned out that Mattie's backyard did not have the right minerals for growing. She never researched and never bought the right kind of soil or fertilizer to add to her yard. She barely looked at the seed packets she bought. Most of them, she planted too late. Mattie also ended up spending more on her water utility bill than she would have saved at the grocery store. Not only did she over-water, but she watered on days that it also rained. She effectively drowned most of her seedlings.

Today, Mattie's backyard is a virtual self-sustaining farm. After her first failure, she did not give up, but she changed one thing. She started from a place of peace. She had patience and learned what needed to be done. Now, she feeds her family a variety of vegetables and even added a chicken coup.

You have already dealt with your past. Face your future with calm and assurance. Calm means patience. Do not forget that God's time is not our time. And know that God is ready for you. Are you ready for Him?

Assignment Number 7

Make a list of things that bring you peace. Include things of beauty that you have seen in your life, or that you are seeing for the first time with your new clarity.

Journal

Journal

Journal

Journal

Journal

CHAPTER EIGHT

A MATTER OF TIME

Most of you reading this book have no doubt. Still, some of you may have questions: Is God real? Is He watching me? Is this journal going to work?

If you do have any doubts, flip back through the pages of this book. Take a look at the things you've written in the preceding pages. There, in your own handwriting is the evidence. Could you have done all that on your own?

As you've worked your way through these chapters and their messages, you should also be able to see that God has been with you every step of the way.

Still not there yet? Don't worry.

Worry? That's one thing you're grateful that you're no longer doing, right?

So, what have you been going through recently, while reading these chapters? We're not talking about your personal situation...everyone's is different. But there is something that you and everyone else experiencing difficult times goes through. It can be found in 100% of every situation we, as humans, face. It was true in ancient times as much as it is today and will be tomorrow. What is it?

Time.

Time is the one thing that God gives you. Admit it. Everyone wishes they had more of it on their last day. They don't wish for more money, more things, more people....they simply want more time. Whether you believe that God is real now or you never believed or you will soon believe, you are going through *time* as you deal with your situation. Time that God has given you, otherwise you'd be gone already.

You already understand that God does not have to answer *why*. The phrase, "it takes time" is also not a very satisfying answer for your situation.

Satisfying or not, it is nonetheless a true answer. Whatever your personal situation may be, the final answer is *time.*

Let's revisit David and his situation. Remember, he had what he thought was an idyllic life and was well on the way to what he believed would be contentment and lifelong happiness. Then as tragically as a death in the family or catastrophic illness diagnosis, his life changed for, what he thought, was the worst. His wife, the centerpiece of his idyllic life, left for a reason he could not understand. David's life was in shambles.

We've already looked at some of the means and situations that David used to work through his tragedy. Let's take a look at his desire for a *quick fix.*

As we look at David's situation again, spend some time and compare it to yours, whatever it is. Because the answer that David got will be the same for you, regardless of the details. And God will be right there with you every step of the way, you'll see.

As with all tragedies, big or small, the immediate task at hand is, and always will be, to make things right again.

What's the first thing we do when a hurricane or other natural disaster strikes? We go to the aid of the injured parties. We immediately send in relief supplies, medical help and other efforts intended to stabilize the situation. When we learn of a serious illness, we seek the best medical advice and care that we can. When we come upon a bad car accident, we extricate the injured parties and send them for help.

The list can go on: fire, flood, unemployment. Whatever the bad situation, whether on a personal scale or a wide scale, our reaction, as humans, is always the same.

We move in as quickly as possible, get the injured stabilized and moved to experts who can do the repairs necessary to restore the injured to the previously acceptable state.

So, how about David? What did he do? His situation was very, very personal. It wasn't a tragedy readily visible to friends and neighbors. It wasn't something that showed on the outside. It really wasn't something that he needed to be rushed anywhere for repairs. So what could he do?

Through David's job, he met many different types of people. He became acquainted with some aspect of their personal lives. So, David started to look around for someone who had endured the same tragic loss as he was going through. After all, if our personal tragedy called for medical help, wouldn't we seek a doctor? If our tragedy was that our home had been destroyed, wouldn't we seek a construction expert? So, David looked for an *expert* in his personal type of tragedy.

As God made his plan for you, he arranged to bring all of the people you will ever need into your life. David certainly was not thinking about that when he remembered the personal story of another man he knew.

"Bob," David said out loud, as he sat at his desk one gloomy day.

Bob was a police lieutenant. David had come to know him through his association at his job. The two men were friendly, having taken lunches together and occasionally attended a baseball game or other sporting event together.

David remembered hearing that Bob had gone through a messy divorce from his first wife, with whom he was married to for ten years. "When was that?" David tried to remember exactly. "It had to have been in the last few years or so."

David realized that Bob had lived through a similar situation. He knew that Bob was doing fine. He even heard that Bob was planning to remarry. And on top of that, Bob had recently been promoted to the rank of Captain. So he must have *the* answer.

David headed over to Bob's office, feeling very confident that his tragic situation was going to come to a swift end. Bob greeted him and was agreeable to telling him all about his personal situation.

"I want the magic pill," David said. "You made it through OK, so you must have the answer."

Bob proceeded to tell David about the breakup with his wife. It was, in fact, similar, but actually much worse than David's breakup. Bob explained that one evening, three years earlier; he came home from the police department and found his wife with another man. Bob pulled his service revolver and chased the half-naked man two blocks before over-taking him.

"I had my service revolver to the guy's head. It almost cost me my job," Bob told David. "All I could think about was blowing this guy away. How could she do this to me?"

But, as swiftly as he had pulled his gun, he stood, replaced it in its holster and he walked away. He walked back to his house, without a word, to his ashamed and crying wife He packed a suitcase and left. He never returned.

"That's terrible," David agreed. "But, you're doing fine now. Everything turned out great. What's the answer? Give it to me."

"Time," Bob said.

"What?" asked David.

"It took what felt like a long time to put my life back together. I even had to visit the staff psychologist and spent many hours with my pastor. The other guy never pressed charges for assault, but he did testify to my actions in the divorce proceedings. The judge granted the divorce, but I was left with only my job and barely that," explained Bob.

Time.

God pulled Bob off the man. God spared Bob from a completely wrecked life in prison. God was there for Bob...and He is there for you.

Still, how could that be the answer? That was a very hollow, unfulfilling answer and not the one David wanted for sure. David almost screamed at his friend to give him the *real* answer. He wanted his hurt to go away.

"It takes time," was Bob's calm response.

So, at that moment, David stormed out of his friend's office, mad at his friend for not helping him. But, did he help him? David went looking elsewhere for *the* answer. And, guess what? Over *time*, he found it.

When David's *time* was up, he, indeed, had *the* answer and it was *time*. Time to evaluate. Time to think. Time to seek. Time to reason. Time to be grateful. Time to forgive. Time. David made it though. Bob made it through...and so will you.

Remember...THERE IS NO QUICK FIX.

Assignment Number 8

Fill these next few pages with every situation in your life where you now know that time was your friend and simply all that you needed to get from a bad place to a good one. Things you would have missed in your life had you not taken time. Here's your free one.

I'm grateful for the time I've had to read this book.

I am grateful for the time...

Journal

Journal

Journal

Journal

Journal

CHAPTER NINE

MOVING ON

Here is a personal prayer that you can turn to in almost any situation:

> *Lord, I ask for clarity at this moment.*
> *I give thanks for all that You have given me.*
> *I am Your servant and carry Your glory out into the world.*
> *Thy will be done.*

Before we finish this last chapter, does this book feel heavier than when you started? It should. If you completed each chapter, then you laid a lot of heavy things onto these pages. The good thing about having a heavy book is that the person holding it should be much lighter, but also much stronger. You have set yourself free one page at a time.

Forgiving yourself, forgiving others and asking their forgiveness laid the ground work. Through giving and acceptance, you have renewed your gratitude. God is there to help. He will listen to your woes and carry you through. The only thing He asks in return is for your thanks. Call it worship or praise, but at its core, it is simply saying, "Thank You".

In *Jeremiah 29:11*, we are told, "For I know the thoughts that I think toward you, says the LORD, thoughts of peace and not of evil, to give you a future and a hope."

The Lord does have a plan for us all. It is not our job to second-guess it or circumvent it. It is our job to be thankful. Keep that attitude and you will be able to move on from that old life.

Gratitude Renewed ultimately consists of four things: Forgiveness, Charity, Acceptance and Peace.

With your new attitude, you are free. You have freed yourself from the past. That means the mistakes you made and the people you wronged. No one on this Earth is perfect, but realizing that is a great step toward being a better person. We have all made mistakes and we will make more in the future. Being able to forgive each other will help us through that. You have freed yourself from yourself.

Sometimes, the worst things we do are to ourselves. We hold ourselves back in our minds and hearts. We punish ourselves for transgressions beyond man's law or even God's. Accepting that we are not perfect and accepting the good and bad in our lives frees us from those misguided thoughts.

You have lastly freed yourself from being negative. Knowing that God is always with you gives you strength. Understanding how to accept and deal with challenges gives you peace. If God never gives you more than you can handle, then what reason is there for negativity?

Once you have moved on from your old life to a gracious new one, it is time to start thinking about another form of moving on.

You must prepare yourself to move on from this physical world to your salvation.

We only exist on this planet for a cosmic moment. It is an inevitability that we will someday become something else. That does not mean to give up and wait to die. It only means that if you live a life of gratitude, you will be well prepared when the moment of your salvation comes.

Believing in God and giving thanks is not an insurance policy. It is a way of life. You don't worship Him "just in case" some other religion got it wrong. You have to have confidence in what comes next. It will give you greater peace and allow for a better life now.

Assignment Number 9

For your final list, write what you are free from or write about your future. Where will your renewed gratitude take you?

Journal

Journal

Journal

Journal

Journal

ENDORSEMENTS

"This book speaks to life on the other side of why? *Beyond the* why do bad things happen to good people? why am I going through this?, why do problems exist?, *lies the answer to joy, peace, gratitude and forgiveness. In this book, you will learn how to let go of the questions and grasp the concept that God wants us to be free from the shackles of* why. *Putting the principles from the book into action will renew the gratitude and help you discover the blessings in your life. I recommend this book to any individual that wants to live on the other side of* why *in a land called peace."*

Mark Payne, Pastor
No Limits Church, Lake Mary, FL

"It is well written and easy to understand and is prospectively a great self-help tool."

Theda Sturm, M.S., L.M.F.T.
In Harmony Counseling

ENDORSEMENTS (*continued*)

"Mark and De have a great gift in writing given to them by God. What a blessing...from God."

Gilbert Remington
Appointee Minister, Semi-Retired
Community of Christ Church

"A beautiful and healing journal. It is an inspired gift of love to all who receive it and start their journeys."

Susan O'Gara
Script Consultant
Lazarus Filmworks

ABOUT THE AUTHORS

De Miller, a former newspaperman, has been writing for three decades. Since moving to Florida, he has become a Christian and devoted much of his writing time to Christian endeavors. He has written and directed several Christian movies and several short films. More info can be found at
www.LazarusFilmworks.com.

Mark Miller currently resides in Florida with his wife and four children. He has achieved some success as a Kindle Best Seller and having one of his short stories selected as a winner in the Florida Writer's Association Short Story Collection.

Mark has written numerous novels, screenplays, short stories and digital series. Many of his stories are geared for the classroom. He has explored his spirituality, writing both with his father and daughter. Inspirational stories with positive messages are his goal with everything he writes.

ABOUT THIS BOOK

This is not a traditional self-help book. It is a life plan designed to renew gratitude and strengthen faith. The authors of this book are not trained psychologists or ordained clergy. They are a father and son with a combined one hundred years (plus) experience of Life. They have faced challenges, experienced failure and explored their faith.

There are several *journal* pages included at the end of each chapter. They are intentionally left blank for you, the reader, to fill.

As seen in the motion picture *God, Where Are You?* (Starring Wade Williams and Kibwe Dorsey, written and directed by De Miller).

Made in the USA
Las Vegas, NV
11 February 2022